KJV ILLUMINATED BIBLE
The Book of Proverbs

The Book of **PROVERBS**

The Book of PROVERBS

Proverbs 1

1 The proverbs of Solomon the son of David, king of Israel;

2 To know wisdom and instruction; to perceive the words of understanding;

3 To receive the instruction of wisdom, justice, and judgment, and equity;

4 To give subtilty to the simple, to the young man knowledge and discretion.

5 A wise [man] will hear, and will increase learning; and a man of understanding shall attain unto wise counsels:

6 To understand a proverb, and the interpretation; the words of the wise, and their dark sayings.

7 The fear of the LORD [is] the beginning of knowledge: [but] fools despise wisdom and instruction.

8 My son, hear the instruction of thy father, and forsake not the law of thy mother:

9 For they [shall be] an ornament of grace unto thy head, and chains about thy neck.

10 My son, if sinners entice thee, consent thou not.

11 If they say, Come with us, let us lay wait for blood, let us lurk privily for the innocent without cause:

12 Let us swallow them up alive as the grave; and whole, as those that go down into the pit:

13 We shall find all precious substance, we shall fill our houses with spoil:

14 Cast in thy lot among us; let us all have one purse:
15 My son, walk not thou in the way with them; refrain thy foot from their path:
16 For their feet run to evil, and make haste to shed blood.
17 Surely in vain the net is spread in the sight of any bird.
18 And they lay wait for their [own] blood; they lurk privily for their [own] lives.
19 So [are] the ways of every one that is greedy of gain; [which] taketh away the life of the owners thereof.
20 Wisdom crieth without; she uttereth her voice in the streets:
21 She crieth in the chief place of concourse, in the openings of the gates: in the city she uttereth her words, [saying],
22 How long, ye simple ones, will ye love simplicity? and the scorners delight in their scorning, and fools hate knowledge?
23 Turn you at my reproof: behold, I will pour out my spirit unto you, I will make known my words unto you.
24 Because I have called, and ye refused; I have stretched out my hand, and no man regarded;
25 But ye have set at nought all my counsel, and would none of my reproof:
26 I also will laugh at your calamity; I will mock when your fear cometh;

27 When your fear cometh as desolation, and your destruction cometh as a whirlwind; when distress and anguish cometh upon you.
28 Then shall they call upon me, but I will not answer; they shall seek me early, but they shall not find me:
29 For that they hated knowledge, and did not choose the fear of the LORD:
30 They would none of my counsel: they despised all my reproof.
31 Therefore shall they eat of the fruit of their own way, and be filled with their own devices.
32 For the turning away of the simple shall slay them, and the prosperity of fools shall destroy them.
33 But whoso hearkeneth unto me shall dwell safely, and shall be quiet from fear of evil.

Proverbs 2

1 My son, if thou wilt receive my words, and hide my commandments with thee;
2 So that thou incline thine ear unto wisdom, [and] apply thine heart to understanding;
3 Yea, if thou criest after knowledge, [and] liftest up thy voice for understanding;
4 If thou seekest her as silver, and searchest for her as [for] hid treasures;
5 Then shalt thou understand the fear of the LORD, and find the knowledge of God.
6 For the LORD giveth wisdom: out of his mouth [cometh] knowledge and understanding.

7 He layeth up sound wisdom for the righteous: [he
is] a buckler to them that walk uprightly.
8 He keepeth the paths of judgment, and preserveth
the way of his saints.
9 Then shalt thou understand righteousness, and
judgment, and equity; [yea], every good path.
10 When wisdom entereth into thine heart, and
knowledge is pleasant unto thy soul;
11 Discretion shall preserve thee, understanding
shall keep thee:
12 To deliver thee from the way of the evil [man],
from the man that speaketh froward things;
13 Who leave the paths of uprightness, to walk in
the ways of darkness;
14 Who rejoice to do evil, [and] delight in the
frowardness of the wicked;
15 Whose ways [are] crooked, and [they] froward
in their paths:
16 To deliver thee from the strange woman, [even]
from the stranger [which] flattereth with her words;
17 Which forsaketh the guide of her youth, and
forgetteth the covenant of her God.
18 For her house inclineth unto death, and her
paths unto the dead.
19 None that go unto her return again, neither take
they hold of the paths of life.
20 That thou mayest walk in the way of good [men],
and keep the paths of the righteous.
21 For the upright shall dwell in the land, and the
perfect shall remain in it.

22 But the wicked shall be cut off from the earth,
and the transgressors shall be rooted out of it.

Proverbs 3

1 My son, forget not my law; but let thine heart keep
my commandments:
2 For length of days, and long life, and peace, shall
they add to thee.
3 Let not mercy and truth forsake thee: bind them
about thy neck; write them upon the table of thine
heart:
4 So shalt thou find favour and good understanding
in the sight of God and man.
5 Trust in the LORD with all thine heart; and lean
not unto thine own understanding.
6 In all thy ways acknowledge him, and he shall direct
thy paths.
7 Be not wise in thine own eyes: fear the LORD, and
depart from evil.
8 It shall be health to thy navel, and marrow to thy
bones.
9 Honour the LORD with thy substance, and with
the firstfruits of all thine increase:
10 So shall thy barns be filled with plenty, and thy
presses shall burst out with new wine.
11 My son, despise not the chastening of the
LORD; neither be weary of his correction:
12 For whom the LORD loveth he correcteth; even
as a father the son [in whom] he delighteth.
13 Happy [is] the man [that] findeth wisdom, and

the man [that] getteth understanding.
14 For the merchandise of it [is] better than the merchandise of silver, and the gain thereof than fine gold.
15 She [is] more precious than rubies: and all the things thou canst desire are not to be compared unto her.
16 Length of days [is] in her right hand; [and] in her left hand riches and honour.
17 Her ways [are] ways of pleasantness, and all her paths [are] peace.
18 She [is] a tree of life to them that lay hold upon her: and happy [is every one] that retaineth her.
19 The LORD by wisdom hath founded the earth; by understanding hath he established the heavens.
20 By his knowledge the depths are broken up, and the clouds drop down the dew.
21 My son, let not them depart from thine eyes: keep sound wisdom and discretion:
22 So shall they be life unto thy soul, and grace to thy neck.
23 Then shalt thou walk in thy way safely, and thy foot shall not stumble.
24 When thou liest down, thou shalt not be afraid: yea, thou shalt lie down, and thy sleep shall be sweet.
25 Be not afraid of sudden fear, neither of the desolation of the wicked, when it cometh.
26 For the LORD shall be thy confidence, and shall keep thy foot from being taken.
27 Withhold not good from them to whom it is

due, when it is in the power of thine hand to do [it].
28 Say not unto thy neighbour, Go, and come again,
and to morrow I will give; when thou hast it by thee.
29 Devise not evil against thy neighbour, seeing he
dwelleth securely by thee.
30 Strive not with a man without cause, if he have
done thee no harm.
31 Envy thou not the oppressor, and choose none
of his ways.
32 For the froward [is] abomination to the LORD:
but his secret [is] with the righteous.
33 The curse of the LORD [is] in the house of the
wicked: but he blesseth the habitation of the just.
34 Surely he scorneth the scorners: but he giveth
grace unto the lowly.
35 The wise shall inherit glory: but shame shall be
the promotion of fools.

Proverbs 4

1 Hear, ye children, the instruction of a father, and
attend to know understanding.
2 For I give you good doctrine, forsake ye not my
law.
3 For I was my father's son, tender and only
[beloved] in the sight of my mother.
4 He taught me also, and said unto me, Let thine
heart retain my words: keep my commandments, and
live.
5 Get wisdom, get understanding: forget [it] not;
neither decline from the words of my mouth.

6 Forsake her not, and she shall preserve thee: love her, and she shall keep thee.

7 Wisdom [is] the principal thing; [therefore] get wisdom: and with all thy getting get understanding.

8 Exalt her, and she shall promote thee: she shall bring thee to honour, when thou dost embrace her.

9 She shall give to thine head an ornament of grace: a crown of glory shall she deliver to thee.

10 Hear, O my son, and receive my sayings; and the years of thy life shall be many.

11 I have taught thee in the way of wisdom; I have led thee in right paths.

12 When thou goest, thy steps shall not be straitened; and when thou runnest, thou shalt not stumble.

13 Take fast hold of instruction; let [her] not go: keep her; for she [is] thy life.

14 Enter not into the path of the wicked, and go not in the way of evil [men].

15 Avoid it, pass not by it, turn from it, and pass away.

16 For they sleep not, except they have done mischief; and their sleep is taken away, unless they cause [some] to fall.

17 For they eat the bread of wickedness, and drink the wine of violence.

18 But the path of the just [is] as the shining light, that shineth more and more unto the perfect day.

19 The way of the wicked [is] as darkness: they know not at what they stumble.

20 My son, attend to my words; incline thine ear unto my sayings.
21 Let them not depart from thine eyes; keep them in the midst of thine heart.
22 For they [are] life unto those that find them, and health to all their flesh.
23 Keep thy heart with all diligence; for out of it [are] the issues of life.
24 Put away from thee a froward mouth, and perverse lips put far from thee.
25 Let thine eyes look right on, and let thine eyelids look straight before thee.
26 Ponder the path of thy feet, and let all thy ways be established.
27 Turn not to the right hand nor to the left: remove thy foot from evil.

Proverbs 5

1 My son, attend unto my wisdom, [and] bow thine ear to my understanding:
2 That thou mayest regard discretion, and [that] thy lips may keep knowledge.
3 For the lips of a strange woman drop [as] an honeycomb, and her mouth [is] smoother than oil:
4 But her end is bitter as wormwood, sharp as a twoedged sword.
5 Her feet go down to death; her steps take hold on hell.
6 Lest thou shouldest ponder the path of life, her ways are moveable, [that] thou canst not know

[them].
7 Hear me now therefore, O ye children, and depart
not from the words of my mouth.
8 Remove thy way far from her, and come not nigh
the door of her house:
9 Lest thou give thine honour unto others, and thy
years unto the cruel:
10 Lest strangers be filled with thy wealth; and thy
labours [be] in the house of a stranger;
11 And thou mourn at the last, when thy flesh and
thy body are consumed,
12 And say, How have I hated instruction, and my
heart despised reproof;
13 And have not obeyed the voice of my teachers,
nor inclined mine ear to them that instructed me!
14 I was almost in all evil in the midst of the
congregation and assembly.
15 Drink waters out of thine own cistern, and
running waters out of thine own well.
16 Let thy fountains be dispersed abroad, [and]
rivers of waters in the streets.
17 Let them be only thine own, and not strangers'
with thee.
18 Let thy fountain be blessed: and rejoice with the
wife of thy youth.
19 [Let her be as] the loving hind and pleasant roe;
let her breasts satisfy thee at all times; and be thou
ravished always with her love.
20 And why wilt thou, my son, be ravished with a
strange woman, and embrace the bosom of a

stranger?
21 For the ways of man [are] before the eyes of the LORD, and he pondereth all his goings.
22 His own iniquities shall take the wicked himself, and he shall be holden with the cords of his sins.
23 He shall die without instruction; and in the greatness of his folly he shall go astray.

Proverbs 6

1 My son, if thou be surety for thy friend, [if] thou hast stricken thy hand with a stranger,
2 Thou art snared with the words of thy mouth, thou art taken with the words of thy mouth.
3 Do this now, my son, and deliver thyself, when thou art come into the hand of thy friend; go, humble thyself, and make sure thy friend.
4 Give not sleep to thine eyes, nor slumber to thine eyelids.
5 Deliver thyself as a roe from the hand [of the hunter], and as a bird from the hand of the fowler.
6 Go to the ant, thou sluggard; consider her ways, and be wise:
7 Which having no guide, overseer, or ruler,
8 Provideth her meat in the summer, [and] gathereth her food in the harvest.
9 How long wilt thou sleep, O sluggard? when wilt thou arise out of thy sleep?
10 [Yet] a little sleep, a little slumber, a little folding of the hands to sleep:
11 So shall thy poverty come as one that travelleth,

and thy want as an armed man.
12 A naughty person, a wicked man, walketh with a
froward mouth.
13 He winketh with his eyes, he speaketh with his
feet, he teacheth with his fingers;
14 Frowardness [is] in his heart, he deviseth
mischief continually; he soweth discord.
15 Therefore shall his calamity come suddenly;
suddenly shall he be broken without remedy.
16 These six [things] doth the LORD hate: yea,
seven [are] an abomination unto him:
17 A proud look, a lying tongue, and hands that
shed innocent blood,
18 An heart that deviseth wicked imaginations, feet
that be swift in running to mischief,
19 A false witness [that] speaketh lies, and he that
soweth discord among brethren.
20 My son, keep thy father's commandment, and
forsake not the law of thy mother:
21 Bind them continually upon thine heart, [and] tie
them about thy neck.
22 When thou goest, it shall lead thee; when thou
sleepest, it shall keep thee; and [when] thou awakest,
it shall talk with thee.
23 For the commandment [is] a lamp; and the law
[is] light; and reproofs of instruction [are] the way of
life:
24 To keep thee from the evil woman, from the
flattery of the tongue of a strange woman.
25 Lust not after her beauty in thine heart; neither

let her take thee with her eyelids.
26 For by means of a whorish woman [a man is brought] to a piece of bread: and the adulteress will hunt for the precious life.
27 Can a man take fire in his bosom, and his clothes not be burned?
28 Can one go upon hot coals, and his feet not be burned?
29 So he that goeth in to his neighbour's wife; whosoever toucheth her shall not be innocent.
30 [Men] do not despise a thief, if he steal to satisfy his soul when he is hungry;
31 But [if] he be found, he shall restore sevenfold; he shall give all the substance of his house.
32 [But] whoso committeth adultery with a woman lacketh understanding: he [that] doeth it destroyeth his own soul.
33 A wound and dishonour shall he get; and his reproach shall not be wiped away.
34 For jealousy [is] the rage of a man: therefore he will not spare in the day of vengeance.
35 He will not regard any ransom; neither will he rest content, though thou givest many gifts.

Proverbs 7

1 My son, keep my words, and lay up my commandments with thee.
2 Keep my commandments, and live; and my law as the apple of thine eye.
3 Bind them upon thy fingers, write them upon the

table of thine heart.
4 Say unto wisdom, Thou [art] my sister; and call understanding [thy] kinswoman:
5 That they may keep thee from the strange woman, from the stranger [which] flattereth with her words.
6 For at the window of my house I looked through my casement,
7 And beheld among the simple ones, I discerned among the youths, a young man void of understanding,
8 Passing through the street near her corner; and he went the way to her house,
9 In the twilight, in the evening, in the black and dark night:
10 And, behold, there met him a woman [with] the attire of an harlot, and subtil of heart.
11 (She [is] loud and stubborn; her feet abide not in her house:
12 Now [is she] without, now in the streets, and lieth in wait at every corner.)
13 So she caught him, and kissed him, [and] with an impudent face said unto him,
14 [I have] peace offerings with me; this day have I payed my vows.
15 Therefore came I forth to meet thee, diligently to seek thy face, and I have found thee.
16 I have decked my bed with coverings of tapestry, with carved [works], with fine linen of Egypt.
17 I have perfumed my bed with myrrh, aloes, and cinnamon.

18 Come, let us take our fill of love until the
morning: let us solace ourselves with loves.
19 For the goodman [is] not at home, he is gone a
long journey:
20 He hath taken a bag of money with him, [and]
will come home at the day appointed.
21 With her much fair speech she caused him to
yield, with the flattering of her lips she forced him.
22 He goeth after her straightway, as an ox goeth
to the slaughter, or as a fool to the correction of the
stocks;
23 Till a dart strike through his liver; as a bird
hasteth to the snare, and knoweth not that it [is] for
his life.
24 Hearken unto me now therefore, O ye children,
and attend to the words of my mouth.
25 Let not thine heart decline to her ways, go not
astray in her paths.
26 For she hath cast down many wounded: yea,
many strong [men] have been slain by her.
27 Her house [is] the way to hell, going down to
the chambers of death.

Proverbs 8

1 Doth not wisdom cry? and understanding put forth
her voice?
2 She standeth in the top of high places, by the way
in the places of the paths.
3 She crieth at the gates, at the entry of the city, at
the coming in at the doors.

4 Unto you, O men, I call; and my voice [is] to the
sons of man.
5 O ye simple, understand wisdom: and, ye fools, be
ye of an understanding heart.
6 Hear; for I will speak of excellent things; and the
opening of my lips [shall be] right things.
7 For my mouth shall speak truth; and wickedness
[is] an abomination to my lips.
8 All the words of my mouth [are] in righteousness;
[there is] nothing froward or perverse in them.
9 They [are] all plain to him that understandeth, and
right to them that find knowledge.
10 Receive my instruction, and not silver; and
knowledge rather than choice gold.
11 For wisdom [is] better than rubies; and all the
things that may be desired are not to be compared
to it.
12 I wisdom dwell with prudence, and find out
knowledge of witty inventions.
13 The fear of the LORD [is] to hate evil: pride, and
arrogancy, and the evil way, and the froward mouth,
do I hate.
14 Counsel [is] mine, and sound wisdom: I [am]
understanding; I have strength.
15 By me kings reign, and princes decree justice.
16 By me princes rule, and nobles, [even] all the
judges of the earth.
17 I love them that love me; and those that seek me
early shall find me.

18 Riches and honour [are] with me; [yea], durable
riches and righteousness.
19 My fruit [is] better than gold, yea, than fine gold;
and my revenue than choice silver.
20 I lead in the way of righteousness, in the midst
of the paths of judgment:
21 That I may cause those that love me to inherit
substance; and I will fill their treasures.
22 The LORD possessed me in the beginning of his
way, before his works of old.
23 I was set up from everlasting, from the beginning,
or ever the earth was.
24 When [there were] no depths, I was brought
forth; when [there were] no fountains abounding
with water.
25 Before the mountains were settled, before the
hills was I brought forth:
26 While as yet he had not made the earth, nor the
fields, nor the highest part of the dust of the world.
27 When he prepared the heavens, I [was] there:
when he set a compass upon the face of the depth:
28 When he established the clouds above: when he
strengthened the fountains of the deep:
29 When he gave to the sea his decree, that the
waters should not pass his commandment: when he
appointed the foundations of the earth:
30 Then I was by him, [as] one brought up [with
him]: and I was daily [his] delight, rejoicing always
before him;

31 Rejoicing in the habitable part of his earth; and
my delights [were] with the sons of men.
32 Now therefore hearken unto me, O ye children:
for blessed [are they that] keep my ways.
33 Hear instruction, and be wise, and refuse it not.
34 Blessed [is] the man that heareth me, watching
daily at my gates, waiting at the posts of my doors.
35 For whoso findeth me findeth life, and shall
obtain favour of the LORD.
36 But he that sinneth against me wrongeth his own
soul: all they that hate me love death.

Proverbs 9

1 Wisdom hath builded her house, she hath hewn
out her seven pillars:
2 She hath killed her beasts; she hath mingled her
wine; she hath also furnished her table.
3 She hath sent forth her maidens: she crieth upon
the highest places of the city,
4 Whoso [is] simple, let him turn in hither: [as for]
him that wanteth understanding, she saith to him,
5 Come, eat of my bread, and drink of the wine
[which] I have mingled.
6 Forsake the foolish, and live; and go in the way of
understanding.
7 He that reproveth a scorner getteth to himself
shame: and he that rebuketh a wicked [man getteth]
himself a blot.
8 Reprove not a scorner, lest he hate thee: rebuke a
wise man, and he will love thee.

9 Give [instruction] to a wise [man], and he will be yet wiser: teach a just [man], and he will increase in learning.
10 The fear of the LORD [is] the beginning of wisdom: and the knowledge of the holy [is] understanding.
11 For by me thy days shall be multiplied, and the years of thy life shall be increased.
12 If thou be wise, thou shalt be wise for thyself: but [if] thou scornest, thou alone shalt bear [it].
13 A foolish woman [is] clamorous: [she is] simple, and knoweth nothing.
14 For she sitteth at the door of her house, on a seat in the high places of the city,
15 To call passengers who go right on their ways:
16 Whoso [is] simple, let him turn in hither: and [as for] him that wanteth understanding, she saith to him,
17 Stolen waters are sweet, and bread [eaten] in secret is pleasant.
18 But he knoweth not that the dead [are] there; [and that] her guests [are] in the depths of hell.

Proverbs 10

1 The proverbs of Solomon. A wise son maketh a glad father: but a foolish son [is] the heaviness of his mother.
2 Treasures of wickedness profit nothing: but righteousness delivereth from death.
3 The LORD will not suffer the soul of the righteous to famish: but he casteth away the substance of the

wicked.

4 He becometh poor that dealeth [with] a slack hand: but the hand of the diligent maketh rich.

5 He that gathereth in summer [is] a wise son: [but] he that sleepeth in harvest [is] a son that causeth shame.

6 Blessings [are] upon the head of the just: but violence covereth the mouth of the wicked.

7 The memory of the just [is] blessed: but the name of the wicked shall rot.

8 The wise in heart will receive commandments: but a prating fool shall fall.

9 He that walketh uprightly walketh surely: but he that perverteth his ways shall be known.

10 He that winketh with the eye causeth sorrow: but a prating fool shall fall.

11 The mouth of a righteous [man is] a well of life: but violence covereth the mouth of the wicked.

12 Hatred stirreth up strifes: but love covereth all sins.

13 In the lips of him that hath understanding wisdom is found: but a rod [is] for the back of him that is void of understanding.

14 Wise [men] lay up knowledge: but the mouth of the foolish [is] near destruction.

15 The rich man's wealth [is] his strong city: the destruction of the poor [is] their poverty.

16 The labour of the righteous [tendeth] to life: the fruit of the wicked to sin.

17 He [is in] the way of life that keepeth instruction:
but he that refuseth reproof erreth.
18 He that hideth hatred [with] lying lips, and he
that uttereth a slander, [is] a fool.
19 In the multitude of words there wanteth not sin:
but he that refraineth his lips [is] wise.
20 The tongue of the just [is as] choice silver: the
heart of the wicked [is] little worth.
21 The lips of the righteous feed many: but fools die
for want of wisdom.
22 The blessing of the LORD, it maketh rich, and
he addeth no sorrow with it.
23 [It is] as sport to a fool to do mischief: but a man
of understanding hath wisdom.
24 The fear of the wicked, it shall come upon him:
but the desire of the righteous shall be granted.
25 As the whirlwind passeth, so [is] the wicked no
[more]: but the righteous [is] an everlasting
foundation.
26 As vinegar to the teeth, and as smoke to the
eyes, so [is] the sluggard to them that send him.
27 The fear of the LORD prolongeth days: but the
years of the wicked shall be shortened.
28 The hope of the righteous [shall be] gladness:
but the expectation of the wicked shall perish.
29 The way of the LORD [is] strength to the
upright: but destruction [shall be] to the workers of
iniquity.
30 The righteous shall never be removed: but the
wicked shall not inhabit the earth.

31 The mouth of the just bringeth forth wisdom: but the froward tongue shall be cut out.

32 The lips of the righteous know what is acceptable: but the mouth of the wicked [speaketh] frowardness.

Proverbs 11

1 A false balance [is] abomination to the LORD: but a just weight [is] his delight.

2 [When] pride cometh, then cometh shame: but with the lowly [is] wisdom.

3 The integrity of the upright shall guide them: but the perverseness of transgressors shall destroy them.

4 Riches profit not in the day of wrath: but righteousness delivereth from death.

5 The righteousness of the perfect shall direct his way: but the wicked shall fall by his own wickedness.

6 The righteousness of the upright shall deliver them: but transgressors shall be taken in [their own] naughtiness.

7 When a wicked man dieth, [his] expectation shall perish: and the hope of unjust [men] perisheth.

8 The righteous is delivered out of trouble, and the wicked cometh in his stead.

9 An hypocrite with [his] mouth destroyeth his neighbour: but through knowledge shall the just be delivered.

10 When it goeth well with the righteous, the city rejoiceth: and when the wicked perish, [there is] shouting.

11 By the blessing of the upright the city is exalted: but it is overthrown by the mouth of the wicked.
12 He that is void of wisdom despiseth his neighbour: but a man of understanding holdeth his peace.
13 A talebearer revealeth secrets: but he that is of a faithful spirit concealeth the matter.
14 Where no counsel [is], the people fall: but in the multitude of counsellors [there is] safety.
15 He that is surety for a stranger shall smart [for it]: and he that hateth suretiship is sure.
16 A gracious woman retaineth honour: and strong [men] retain riches.
17 The merciful man doeth good to his own soul: but [he that is] cruel troubleth his own flesh.
18 The wicked worketh a deceitful work: but to him that soweth righteousness [shall be] a sure reward.
19 As righteousness [tendeth] to life: so he that pursueth evil [pursueth it] to his own death.
20 They that are of a froward heart [are] abomination to the LORD: but [such as are] upright in [their] way [are] his delight.
21 [Though] hand [join] in hand, the wicked shall not be unpunished: but the seed of the righteous shall be delivered.
22 [As] a jewel of gold in a swine's snout, [so is] a fair woman which is without discretion.
23 The desire of the righteous [is] only good: [but] the expectation of the wicked [is] wrath.

24 There is that scattereth, and yet increaseth; and
[there is] that withholdeth more than is meet, but [it
tendeth] to poverty.
25 The liberal soul shall be made fat: and he that
watereth shall be watered also himself.
26 He that withholdeth corn, the people shall curse
him: but blessing [shall be] upon the head of him that
selleth [it].
27 He that diligently seeketh good procureth
favour: but he that seeketh mischief, it shall come
unto him.
28 He that trusteth in his riches shall fall: but the
righteous shall flourish as a branch.
29 He that troubleth his own house shall inherit the
wind: and the fool [shall be] servant to the wise of
heart.
30 The fruit of the righteous [is] a tree of life; and
he that winneth souls [is] wise.
31 Behold, the righteous shall be recompensed in
the earth: much more the wicked and the sinner.

Proverbs 12

1 Whoso loveth instruction loveth knowledge: but
he that hateth reproof [is] brutish.
2 A good [man] obtaineth favour of the LORD: but
a man of wicked devices will he condemn.
3 A man shall not be established by wickedness: but
the root of the righteous shall not be moved.
4 A virtuous woman [is] a crown to her husband: but
she that maketh ashamed [is] as rottenness in his

bones.
5 The thoughts of the righteous [are] right: [but] the counsels of the wicked [are] deceit.
6 The words of the wicked [are] to lie in wait for blood: but the mouth of the upright shall deliver them.
7 The wicked are overthrown, and [are] not: but the house of the righteous shall stand.
8 A man shall be commended according to his wisdom: but he that is of a perverse heart shall be despised.
9 [He that is] despised, and hath a servant, [is] better than he that honoureth himself, and lacketh bread.
10 A righteous [man] regardeth the life of his beast: but the tender mercies of the wicked [are] cruel.
11 He that tilleth his land shall be satisfied with bread: but he that followeth vain [persons is] void of understanding.
12 The wicked desireth the net of evil [men]: but the root of the righteous yieldeth [fruit].
13 The wicked is snared by the transgression of [his] lips: but the just shall come out of trouble.
14 A man shall be satisfied with good by the fruit of [his] mouth: and the recompence of a man's hands shall be rendered unto him.
15 The way of a fool [is] right in his own eyes: but he that hearkeneth unto counsel [is] wise.
16 A fool's wrath is presently known: but a prudent [man] covereth shame.

17 [He that] speaketh truth sheweth forth righteousness: but a false witness deceit.
18 There is that speaketh like the piercings of a sword: but the tongue of the wise [is] health.
19 The lip of truth shall be established for ever: but a lying tongue [is] but for a moment.
20 Deceit [is] in the heart of them that imagine evil: but to the counsellors of peace [is] joy.
21 There shall no evil happen to the just: but the wicked shall be filled with mischief.
22 Lying lips [are] abomination to the LORD: but they that deal truly [are] his delight.
23 A prudent man concealeth knowledge: but the heart of fools proclaimeth foolishness.
24 The hand of the diligent shall bear rule: but the slothful shall be under tribute.
25 Heaviness in the heart of man maketh it stoop: but a good word maketh it glad.
26 The righteous [is] more excellent than his neighbour: but the way of the wicked seduceth them.
27 The slothful [man] roasteth not that which he took in hunting: but the substance of a diligent man [is] precious.
28 In the way of righteousness [is] life; and [in] the pathway [thereof there is] no death.

Proverbs 13

1 A wise son [heareth] his father's instruction: but a scorner heareth not rebuke.

2 A man shall eat good by the fruit of [his] mouth: but the soul of the transgressors [shall eat] violence.
3 He that keepeth his mouth keepeth his life: [but] he that openeth wide his lips shall have destruction.
4 The soul of the sluggard desireth, and [hath] nothing: but the soul of the diligent shall be made fat.
5 A righteous [man] hateth lying: but a wicked [man] is loathsome, and cometh to shame.
6 Righteousness keepeth [him that is] upright in the way: but wickedness overthroweth the sinner.
7 There is that maketh himself rich, yet [hath] nothing: [there is] that maketh himself poor, yet [hath] great riches.
8 The ransom of a man's life [are] his riches: but the poor heareth not rebuke.
9 The light of the righteous rejoiceth: but the lamp of the wicked shall be put out.
10 Only by pride cometh contention: but with the well advised [is] wisdom.
11 Wealth [gotten] by vanity shall be diminished: but he that gathereth by labour shall increase.
12 Hope deferred maketh the heart sick: but [when] the desire cometh, [it is] a tree of life.
13 Whoso despiseth the word shall be destroyed: but he that feareth the commandment shall be rewarded.
14 The law of the wise [is] a fountain of life, to depart from the snares of death.
15 Good understanding giveth favour: but the way of transgressors [is] hard.

16 Every prudent [man] dealeth with knowledge: but a fool layeth open [his] folly.
17 A wicked messenger falleth into mischief: but a faithful ambassador [is] health.
18 Poverty and shame [shall be to] him that refuseth instruction: but he that regardeth reproof shall be honoured.
19 The desire accomplished is sweet to the soul: but [it is] abomination to fools to depart from evil.
20 He that walketh with wise [men] shall be wise: but a companion of fools shall be destroyed.
21 Evil pursueth sinners: but to the righteous good shall be repayed.
22 A good [man] leaveth an inheritance to his children's children: and the wealth of the sinner [is] laid up for the just.
23 Much food [is in] the tillage of the poor: but there is [that is] destroyed for want of judgment.
24 He that spareth his rod hateth his son: but he that loveth him chasteneth him betimes.
25 The righteous eateth to the satisfying of his soul: but the belly of the wicked shall want.

Proverbs 14

1 Every wise woman buildeth her house: but the foolish plucketh it down with her hands.
2 He that walketh in his uprightness feareth the LORD: but [he that is] perverse in his ways despiseth him.

3 In the mouth of the foolish [is] a rod of pride: but the lips of the wise shall preserve them.
4 Where no oxen [are], the crib [is] clean: but much increase [is] by the strength of the ox.
5 A faithful witness will not lie: but a false witness will utter lies.
6 A scorner seeketh wisdom, and [findeth it] not: but knowledge [is] easy unto him that understandeth.
7 Go from the presence of a foolish man, when thou perceivest not [in him] the lips of knowledge.
8 The wisdom of the prudent [is] to understand his way: but the folly of fools [is] deceit.
9 Fools make a mock at sin: but among the righteous [there is] favour.
10 The heart knoweth his own bitterness; and a stranger doth not intermeddle with his joy.
11 The house of the wicked shall be overthrown: but the tabernacle of the upright shall flourish.
12 There is a way which seemeth right unto a man, but the end thereof [are] the ways of death.
13 Even in laughter the heart is sorrowful; and the end of that mirth [is] heaviness.
14 The backslider in heart shall be filled with his own ways: and a good man [shall be satisfied] from himself.
15 The simple believeth every word: but the prudent [man] looketh well to his going.
16 A wise [man] feareth, and departeth from evil: but the fool rageth, and is confident.
17 [He that is] soon angry dealeth foolishly: and a

man of wicked devices is hated.
18 The simple inherit folly: but the prudent are
crowned with knowledge.
19 The evil bow before the good; and the wicked
at the gates of the righteous.
20 The poor is hated even of his own neighbour:
but the rich [hath] many friends.
21 He that despiseth his neighbour sinneth: but he
that hath mercy on the poor, happy [is] he.
22 Do they not err that devise evil? but mercy and
truth [shall be] to them that devise good.
23 In all labour there is profit: but the talk of the
lips [tendeth] only to penury.
24 The crown of the wise [is] their riches: [but] the
foolishness of fools [is] folly.
25 A true witness delivereth souls: but a deceitful
[witness] speaketh lies.
26 In the fear of the LORD [is] strong confidence:
and his children shall have a place of refuge.
27 The fear of the LORD [is] a fountain of life, to
depart from the snares of death.
28 In the multitude of people [is] the king's honour:
but in the want of people [is] the destruction of the
prince.
29 [He that is] slow to wrath [is] of great
understanding: but [he that is] hasty of spirit exalteth
folly.
30 A sound heart [is] the life of the flesh: but envy
the rottenness of the bones.
31 He that oppresseth the poor reproacheth his

Maker: but he that honoureth him hath mercy on the poor.

32 The wicked is driven away in his wickedness: but the righteous hath hope in his death.

33 Wisdom resteth in the heart of him that hath understanding: but [that which is] in the midst of fools is made known.

34 Righteousness exalteth a nation: but sin [is] a reproach to any people.

35 The king's favour [is] toward a wise servant: but his wrath is [against] him that causeth shame.

Proverbs 15

1 A soft answer turneth away wrath: but grievous words stir up anger.

2 The tongue of the wise useth knowledge aright: but the mouth of fools poureth out foolishness.

3 The eyes of the LORD [are] in every place, beholding the evil and the good.

4 A wholesome tongue [is] a tree of life: but perverseness therein [is] a breach in the spirit.

5 A fool despiseth his father's instruction: but he that regardeth reproof is prudent.

6 In the house of the righteous [is] much treasure: but in the revenues of the wicked is trouble.

7 The lips of the wise disperse knowledge: but the heart of the foolish [doeth] not so.

8 The sacrifice of the wicked [is] an abomination to the LORD: but the prayer of the upright [is] his delight.

9 The way of the wicked [is] an abomination unto
the LORD: but he loveth him that followeth after
righteousness.
10 Correction [is] grievous unto him that forsaketh
the way: [and] he that hateth reproof shall die.
11 Hell and destruction [are] before the LORD:
how much more then the hearts of the children of
men?
12 A scorner loveth not one that reproveth him:
neither will he go unto the wise.
13 A merry heart maketh a cheerful countenance:
but by sorrow of the heart the spirit is broken.
14 The heart of him that hath understanding
seeketh knowledge: but the mouth of fools feedeth
on foolishness.
15 All the days of the afflicted [are] evil: but he that
is of a merry heart [hath] a continual feast.
16 Better [is] little with the fear of the LORD than
great treasure and trouble therewith.
17 Better [is] a dinner of herbs where love is, than
a stalled ox and hatred therewith.
18 A wrathful man stirreth up strife: but [he that is]
slow to anger appeaseth strife.
19 The way of the slothful [man is] as an hedge of
thorns: but the way of the righteous [is] made plain.
20 A wise son maketh a glad father: but a foolish
man despiseth his mother.
21 Folly [is] joy to [him that is] destitute of wisdom:
but a man of understanding walketh uprightly.
22 Without counsel purposes are disappointed: but

in the multitude of counsellors they are established.
23 A man hath joy by the answer of his mouth: and
a word [spoken] in due season, how good [is it]!
24 The way of life [is] above to the wise, that he
may depart from hell beneath.
25 The LORD will destroy the house of the proud:
but he will establish the border of the widow.
26 The thoughts of the wicked [are] an
abomination
to the LORD: but [the words] of the pure [are]
pleasant
words.
27 He that is greedy of gain troubleth his own
house; but he that hateth gifts shall live.
28 The heart of the righteous studieth to answer:
but the mouth of the wicked poureth out evil things.
29 The LORD [is] far from the wicked: but he
heareth the prayer of the righteous.
30 The light of the eyes rejoiceth the heart: [and] a
good report maketh the bones fat.
31 The ear that heareth the reproof of life abideth
among the wise.
32 He that refuseth instruction despiseth his own
soul: but he that heareth reproof getteth
understanding.
33 The fear of the LORD [is] the instruction of
wisdom; and before honour [is] humility.

Proverbs 16

1 The preparations of the heart in man, and the answer of the tongue, [is] from the LORD.

2 All the ways of a man [are] clean in his own eyes; but the LORD weigheth the spirits.

3 Commit thy works unto the LORD, and thy thoughts shall be established.

4 The LORD hath made all [things] for himself: yea, even the wicked for the day of evil.

5 Every one [that is] proud in heart [is] an abomination to the LORD: [though] hand [join] in hand, he shall not be unpunished.

6 By mercy and truth iniquity is purged: and by the fear of the LORD [men] depart from evil.

7 When a man's ways please the LORD, he maketh even his enemies to be at peace with him.

8 Better [is] a little with righteousness than great revenues without right.

9 A man's heart deviseth his way: but the LORD directeth his steps.

10 A divine sentence [is] in the lips of the king: his mouth transgresseth not in judgment.

11 A just weight and balance [are] the LORD'S: all the weights of the bag [are] his work.

12 [It is] an abomination to kings to commit wickedness: for the throne is established by righteousness.

13 Righteous lips [are] the delight of kings; and they love him that speaketh right.

14 The wrath of a king [is as] messengers of death:
but a wise man will pacify it.
15 In the light of the king's countenance [is] life; and
his favour [is] as a cloud of the latter rain.
16 How much better [is it] to get wisdom than
gold! and to get understanding rather to be chosen
than silver!
17 The highway of the upright [is] to depart from
evil: he that keepeth his way preserveth his soul.
18 Pride [goeth] before destruction, and an haughty
spirit before a fall.
19 Better [it is to be] of an humble spirit with the
lowly, than to divide the spoil with the proud.
20 He that handleth a matter wisely shall find good:
and whoso trusteth in the LORD, happy [is] he.
21 The wise in heart shall be called prudent: and the
sweetness of the lips increaseth learning.
22 Understanding [is] a wellspring of life unto him
that hath it: but the instruction of fools [is] folly.
23 The heart of the wise teacheth his mouth, and
addeth learning to his lips.
24 Pleasant words [are as] an honeycomb, sweet to
the soul, and health to the bones.
25 There is a way that seemeth right unto a man,
but the end thereof [are] the ways of death.
26 He that laboureth laboureth for himself; for his
mouth craveth it of him.
27 An ungodly man diggeth up evil: and in his lips
[there is] as a burning fire.
28 A froward man soweth strife: and a whisperer

separateth chief friends.
29 A violent man enticeth his neighbour, and leadeth him into the way [that is] not good.
30 He shutteth his eyes to devise froward things: moving his lips he bringeth evil to pass.
31 The hoary head [is] a crown of glory, [if] it be found in the way of righteousness.
32 [He that is] slow to anger [is] better than the mighty; and he that ruleth his spirit than he that taketh a city.
33 The lot is cast into the lap; but the whole disposing thereof [is] of the LORD.

Proverbs 17

1 Better [is] a dry morsel, and quietness therewith, than an house full of sacrifices [with] strife.
2 A wise servant shall have rule over a son that causeth shame, and shall have part of the inheritance among the brethren.
3 The fining pot [is] for silver, and the furnace for gold: but the LORD trieth the hearts.
4 A wicked doer giveth heed to false lips; [and] a liar giveth ear to a naughty tongue.
5 Whoso mocketh the poor reproacheth his Maker: [and] he that is glad at calamities shall not be unpunished.
6 Children's children [are] the crown of old men; and the glory of children [are] their fathers.
7 Excellent speech becometh not a fool: much less do lying lips a prince.

8 A gift [is as] a precious stone in the eyes of him
that hath it: whithersoever it turneth, it prospereth.
9 He that covereth a transgression seeketh love; but
he that repeateth a matter separateth [very] friends.
10 A reproof entereth more into a wise man than
an hundred stripes into a fool.
11 An evil [man] seeketh only rebellion: therefore
a cruel messenger shall be sent against him.
12 Let a bear robbed of her whelps meet a man,
rather than a fool in his folly.
13 Whoso rewardeth evil for good, evil shall not
depart from his house.
14 The beginning of strife [is as] when one letteth
out water: therefore leave off contention, before it
be meddled with.
15 He that justifieth the wicked, and he that
condemneth the just, even they both [are]
abomination to the LORD.
16 Wherefore [is there] a price in the hand of a fool
to get wisdom, seeing [he hath] no heart [to it]?
17 A friend loveth at all times, and a brother is born
for adversity.
18 A man void of understanding striketh hands,
[and] becometh surety in the presence of his friend.
19 He loveth transgression that loveth strife: [and]
he that exalteth his gate seeketh destruction.
20 He that hath a froward heart findeth no good:
and he that hath a perverse tongue falleth into
mischief.
21 He that begetteth a fool [doeth it] to his sorrow:

and the father of a fool hath no joy.
22 A merry heart doeth good [like] a medicine: but a broken spirit drieth the bones.
23 A wicked [man] taketh a gift out of the bosom to pervert the ways of judgment.
24 Wisdom [is] before him that hath understanding; but the eyes of a fool [are] in the ends of the earth.
25 A foolish son [is] a grief to his father, and bitterness to her that bare him.
26 Also to punish the just [is] not good, [nor] to strike princes for equity.
27 He that hath knowledge spareth his words: [and] a man of understanding is of an excellent spirit.
28 Even a fool, when he holdeth his peace, is counted wise: [and] he that shutteth his lips [is esteemed] a man of understanding.

Proverbs 18

1 Through desire a man, having separated himself, seeketh [and] intermeddleth with all wisdom.
2 A fool hath no delight in understanding, but that his heart may discover itself.
3 When the wicked cometh, [then] cometh also contempt, and with ignominy reproach.
4 The words of a man's mouth [are as] deep waters, [and] the wellspring of wisdom [as] a flowing brook.
5 [It is] not good to accept the person of the wicked, to overthrow the righteous in judgment.
6 A fool's lips enter into contention, and his mouth

calleth for strokes.
7 A fool's mouth [is] his destruction, and his lips [are] the snare of his soul.
8 The words of a talebearer [are] as wounds, and they go down into the innermost parts of the belly.
9 He also that is slothful in his work is brother to him that is a great waster.
10 The name of the LORD [is] a strong tower: the righteous runneth into it, and is safe.
11 The rich man's wealth [is] his strong city, and as an high wall in his own conceit.
12 Before destruction the heart of man is haughty, and before honour [is] humility.
13 He that answereth a matter before he heareth [it], it [is] folly and shame unto him.
14 The spirit of a man will sustain his infirmity; but a wounded spirit who can bear?
15 The heart of the prudent getteth knowledge; and the ear of the wise seeketh knowledge.
16 A man's gift maketh room for him, and bringeth him before great men.
17 [He that is] first in his own cause [seemeth] just; but his neighbour cometh and searcheth him.
18 The lot causeth contentions to cease, and parteth between the mighty.
19 A brother offended [is harder to be won] than a strong city: and [their] contentions [are] like the bars of a castle.
20 A man's belly shall be satisfied with the fruit of his mouth; [and] with the increase of his lips shall he

be filled.
21 Death and life [are] in the power of the tongue: and they that love it shall eat the fruit thereof.
22 [Whoso] findeth a wife findeth a good [thing], and obtaineth favour of the LORD.
23 The poor useth intreaties; but the rich answereth roughly.
24 A man [that hath] friends must shew himself friendly: and there is a friend [that] sticketh closer than a brother.

Proverbs 19

1 Better [is] the poor that walketh in his integrity, than [he that is] perverse in his lips, and is a fool.
2 Also, [that] the soul [be] without knowledge, [it is] not good; and he that hasteth with [his] feet sinneth.
3 The foolishness of man perverteth his way: and his heart fretteth against the LORD.
4 Wealth maketh many friends; but the poor is separated from his neighbour.
5 A false witness shall not be unpunished, and [he that] speaketh lies shall not escape.
6 Many will intreat the favour of the prince: and every man [is] a friend to him that giveth gifts.
7 All the brethren of the poor do hate him: how much more do his friends go far from him? he pursueth [them with] words, [yet] they [are] wanting [to him].
8 He that getteth wisdom loveth his own soul: he that keepeth understanding shall find good.

9 A false witness shall not be unpunished, and [he that] speaketh lies shall perish.
10 Delight is not seemly for a fool; much less for a servant to have rule over princes.
11 The discretion of a man deferreth his anger; and [it is] his glory to pass over a transgression.
12 The king's wrath [is] as the roaring of a lion; but his favour [is] as dew upon the grass.
13 A foolish son [is] the calamity of his father: and the contentions of a wife [are] a continual dropping.
14 House and riches [are] the inheritance of fathers: and a prudent wife [is] from the LORD.
15 Slothfulness casteth into a deep sleep; and an idle soul shall suffer hunger.
16 He that keepeth the commandment keepeth his own soul; [but] he that despiseth his ways shall die.
17 He that hath pity upon the poor lendeth unto the LORD; and that which he hath given will he pay him again.
18 Chasten thy son while there is hope, and let not thy soul spare for his crying.
19 A man of great wrath shall suffer punishment: for if thou deliver [him], yet thou must do it again.
20 Hear counsel, and receive instruction, that thou mayest be wise in thy latter end.
21 [There are] many devices in a man's heart; nevertheless the counsel of the LORD, that shall stand.
22 The desire of a man [is] his kindness: and a poor man [is] better than a liar.

23 The fear of the LORD [tendeth] to life: and [he that hath it] shall abide satisfied; he shall not be visited with evil.
24 A slothful [man] hideth his hand in [his] bosom, and will not so much as bring it to his mouth again.
25 Smite a scorner, and the simple will beware: and reprove one that hath understanding, [and] he will understand knowledge.
26 He that wasteth [his] father, [and] chaseth away [his] mother, [is] a son that causeth shame, and bringeth reproach.
27 Cease, my son, to hear the instruction [that causeth] to err from the words of knowledge.
28 An ungodly witness scorneth judgment: and the mouth of the wicked devoureth iniquity.
29 Judgments are prepared for scorners, and stripes for the back of fools.

Proverbs 20

1 Wine [is] a mocker, strong drink [is] raging: and whosoever is deceived thereby is not wise.
2 The fear of a king [is] as the roaring of a lion: [whoso] provoketh him to anger sinneth [against] his own soul.
3 [It is] an honour for a man to cease from strife: but every fool will be meddling.
4 The sluggard will not plow by reason of the cold; [therefore] shall he beg in harvest, and [have] nothing.
5 Counsel in the heart of man [is like] deep water;

but a man of understanding will draw it out.
6 Most men will proclaim every one his own goodness: but a faithful man who can find?
7 The just [man] walketh in his integrity: his children [are] blessed after him.
8 A king that sitteth in the throne of judgment scattereth away all evil with his eyes.
9 Who can say, I have made my heart clean, I am pure from my sin?
10 Divers weights, [and] divers measures, both of them [are] alike abomination to the LORD.
11 Even a child is known by his doings, whether his work [be] pure, and whether [it be] right.
12 The hearing ear, and the seeing eye, the LORD hath made even both of them.
13 Love not sleep, lest thou come to poverty; open thine eyes, [and] thou shalt be satisfied with bread.
14 [It is] naught, [it is] naught, saith the buyer: but when he is gone his way, then he boasteth.
15 There is gold, and a multitude of rubies: but the lips of knowledge [are] a precious jewel.
16 Take his garment that is surety [for] a stranger: and take a pledge of him for a strange woman.
17 Bread of deceit [is] sweet to a man; but afterwards his mouth shall be filled with gravel.
18 [Every] purpose is established by counsel: and with good advice make war.
19 He that goeth about [as] a talebearer revealeth secrets: therefore meddle not with him that flattereth with his lips.

20 Whoso curseth his father or his mother, his lamp shall be put out in obscure darkness.

21 An inheritance [may be] gotten hastily at the beginning; but the end thereof shall not be blessed.

22 Say not thou, I will recompense evil; [but] wait on the LORD, and he shall save thee.

23 Divers weights [are] an abomination unto the LORD; and a false balance [is] not good.

24 Man's goings [are] of the LORD; how can a man then understand his own way?

25 [It is] a snare to the man [who] devoureth [that which is] holy, and after vows to make enquiry.

26 A wise king scattereth the wicked, and bringeth the wheel over them.

27 The spirit of man [is] the candle of the LORD, searching all the inward parts of the belly.

28 Mercy and truth preserve the king: and his throne is upholden by mercy.

29 The glory of young men [is] their strength: and the beauty of old men [is] the gray head.

30 The blueness of a wound cleanseth away evil: so [do] stripes the inward parts of the belly.

Proverbs 21

1 The king's heart [is] in the hand of the LORD, [as] the rivers of water: he turneth it whithersoever he will.

2 Every way of a man [is] right in his own eyes: but the LORD pondereth the hearts.

3 To do justice and judgment [is] more acceptable

to the LORD than sacrifice.
4 An high look, and a proud heart, [and] the plowing of the wicked, [is] sin.
5 The thoughts of the diligent [tend] only to plenteousness; but of every one [that is] hasty only to want.
6 The getting of treasures by a lying tongue [is] a vanity tossed to and fro of them that seek death.
7 The robbery of the wicked shall destroy them; because they refuse to do judgment.
8 The way of man [is] froward and strange: but [as for] the pure, his work [is] right.
9 [It is] better to dwell in a corner of the housetop, than with a brawling woman in a wide house.
10 The soul of the wicked desireth evil: his neighbour findeth no favour in his eyes.
11 When the scorner is punished, the simple is made wise: and when the wise is instructed, he receiveth knowledge.
12 The righteous [man] wisely considereth the house of the wicked: [but God] overthroweth the wicked for [their] wickedness.
13 Whoso stoppeth his ears at the cry of the poor, he also shall cry himself, but shall not be heard.
14 A gift in secret pacifieth anger: and a reward in the bosom strong wrath.
15 [It is] joy to the just to do judgment: but destruction [shall be] to the workers of iniquity.
16 The man that wandereth out of the way of understanding shall remain in the congregation of the

dead.
17 He that loveth pleasure [shall be] a poor man: he that loveth wine and oil shall not be rich.
18 The wicked [shall be] a ransom for the righteous, and the transgressor for the upright.
19 [It is] better to dwell in the wilderness, than with a contentious and an angry woman.
20 [There is] treasure to be desired and oil in the dwelling of the wise; but a foolish man spendeth it up.
21 He that followeth after righteousness and mercy findeth life, righteousness, and honour.
22 A wise [man] scaleth the city of the mighty, and casteth down the strength of the confidence thereof.
23 Whoso keepeth his mouth and his tongue keepeth his soul from troubles.
24 Proud [and] haughty scorner [is] his name, who dealeth in proud wrath.
25 The desire of the slothful killeth him; for his hands refuse to labour.
26 He coveteth greedily all the day long: but the righteous giveth and spareth not.
27 The sacrifice of the wicked [is] abomination: how much more, [when] he bringeth it with a wicked mind?
28 A false witness shall perish: but the man that heareth speaketh constantly.
29 A wicked man hardeneth his face: but [as for] the upright, he directeth his way.
30 [There is] no wisdom nor understanding nor counsel against the LORD.

31 The horse [is] prepared against the day of battle: but safety [is] of the LORD.

Proverbs 22

1 A [good] name [is] rather to be chosen than great riches, [and] loving favour rather than silver and gold.
2 The rich and poor meet together: the LORD [is] the maker of them all.
3 A prudent [man] foreseeth the evil, and hideth himself: but the simple pass on, and are punished.
4 By humility [and] the fear of the LORD [are] riches, and honour, and life.
5 Thorns [and] snares [are] in the way of the froward: he that doth keep his soul shall be far from them.
6 Train up a child in the way he should go: and when he is old, he will not depart from it.
7 The rich ruleth over the poor, and the borrower [is] servant to the lender.
8 He that soweth iniquity shall reap vanity: and the rod of his anger shall fail.
9 He that hath a bountiful eye shall be blessed; for he giveth of his bread to the poor.
10 Cast out the scorner, and contention shall go out; yea, strife and reproach shall cease.
11 He that loveth pureness of heart, [for] the grace of his lips the king [shall be] his friend.
12 The eyes of the LORD preserve knowledge, and he overthroweth the words of the transgressor.
13 The slothful [man] saith, [There is] a lion

without, I shall be slain in the streets.
14 The mouth of strange women [is] a deep pit: he that is abhorred of the LORD shall fall therein.
15 Foolishness [is] bound in the heart of a child; [but] the rod of correction shall drive it far from him.
16 He that oppresseth the poor to increase his [riches, and] he that giveth to the rich, [shall] surely [come] to want.
17 Bow down thine ear, and hear the words of the wise, and apply thine heart unto my knowledge.
18 For [it is] a pleasant thing if thou keep them within
thee; they shall withal be fitted in thy lips.
19 That thy trust may be in the LORD, I have made known to thee this day, even to thee.
20 Have not I written to thee excellent things in counsels and knowledge,
21 That I might make thee know the certainty of the words of truth; that thou mightest answer the words of truth to them that send unto thee?
22 Rob not the poor, because he [is] poor: neither oppress the afflicted in the gate:
23 For the LORD will plead their cause, and spoil the soul of those that spoiled them.
24 Make no friendship with an angry man; and with a furious man thou shalt not go:
25 Lest thou learn his ways, and get a snare to thy soul.
26 Be not thou [one] of them that strike hands, [or] of them that are sureties for debts.

27 If thou hast nothing to pay, why should he take away thy bed from under thee?
28 Remove not the ancient landmark, which thy fathers have set.
29 Seest thou a man diligent in his business? he shall stand before kings; he shall not stand before mean [men].

Proverbs 23

1 When thou sittest to eat with a ruler, consider diligently what [is] before thee:
2 And put a knife to thy throat, if thou [be] a man given to appetite.
3 Be not desirous of his dainties: for they [are] deceitful meat.
4 Labour not to be rich: cease from thine own wisdom.
5 Wilt thou set thine eyes upon that which is not? for [riches] certainly make themselves wings; they fly away as an eagle toward heaven.
6 Eat thou not the bread of [him that hath] an evil eye, neither desire thou his dainty meats:
7 For as he thinketh in his heart, so [is] he: Eat and drink, saith he to thee; but his heart [is] not with thee.
8 The morsel [which] thou hast eaten shalt thou vomit up, and lose thy sweet words.
9 Speak not in the ears of a fool: for he will despise the wisdom of thy words.
10 Remove not the old landmark; and enter not

into the fields of the fatherless:
11 For their redeemer [is] mighty; he shall plead their cause with thee.
12 Apply thine heart unto instruction, and thine ears to the words of knowledge.
13 Withhold not correction from the child: for [if] thou beatest him with the rod, he shall not die.
14 Thou shalt beat him with the rod, and shalt deliver his soul from hell.
15 My son, if thine heart be wise, my heart shall rejoice, even mine.
16 Yea, my reins shall rejoice, when thy lips speak right things.
17 Let not thine heart envy sinners: but [be thou] in the fear of the LORD all the day long.
18 For surely there is an end; and thine expectation shall not be cut off.
19 Hear thou, my son, and be wise, and guide thine heart in the way.
20 Be not among winebibbers; among riotous eaters of flesh:
21 For the drunkard and the glutton shall come to poverty: and drowsiness shall clothe [a man] with rags.
22 Hearken unto thy father that begat thee, and despise not thy mother when she is old.
23 Buy the truth, and sell [it] not; [also] wisdom, and instruction, and understanding.
24 The father of the righteous shall greatly rejoice: and he that begetteth a wise [child] shall have joy of

him.
25 Thy father and thy mother shall be glad, and she
that bare thee shall rejoice.
26 My son, give me thine heart, and let thine eyes
observe my ways.
27 For a whore [is] a deep ditch; and a strange
woman [is] a narrow pit.
28 She also lieth in wait as [for] a prey, and
increaseth the transgressors among men.
29 Who hath woe? who hath sorrow? who hath
contentions? who hath babbling? who hath wounds
without cause? who hath redness of eyes?
30 They that tarry long at the wine; they that go to
seek mixed wine.
31 Look not thou upon the wine when it is red,
when it giveth his colour in the cup, [when] it moveth
itself aright.
32 At the last it biteth like a serpent, and stingeth
like an adder.
33 Thine eyes shall behold strange women, and
thine heart shall utter perverse things.
34 Yea, thou shalt be as he that lieth down in the
midst of the sea, or as he that lieth upon the top of a
mast.
35 They have stricken me, [shalt thou say, and] I
was not sick; they have beaten me, [and] I felt [it] not:
when shall I awake? I will seek it yet again.

Proverbs 24

1 Be not thou envious against evil men, neither desire to be with them.

2 For their heart studieth destruction, and their lips talk of mischief.

3 Through wisdom is an house builded; and by understanding it is established:

4 And by knowledge shall the chambers be filled with all precious and pleasant riches.

5 A wise man [is] strong; yea, a man of knowledge increaseth strength.

6 For by wise counsel thou shalt make thy war: and in multitude of counsellors [there is] safety.

7 Wisdom [is] too high for a fool: he openeth not his mouth in the gate.

8 He that deviseth to do evil shall be called a mischievous person.

9 The thought of foolishness [is] sin: and the scorner [is] an abomination to men.

10 [If] thou faint in the day of adversity, thy strength [is] small.

11 If thou forbear to deliver [them that are] drawn unto death, and [those that are] ready to be slain;

12 If thou sayest, Behold, we knew it not; doth not he that pondereth the heart consider [it]? and he that keepeth thy soul, doth [not] he know [it]? and shall [not] he render to [every] man according to his works?

13 My son, eat thou honey, because [it is] good; and

the honeycomb, [which is] sweet to thy taste:
14 So [shall] the knowledge of wisdom [be] unto
thy soul: when thou hast found [it], then there shall
be a reward, and thy expectation shall not be cut off.
15 Lay not wait, O wicked [man], against the
dwelling of the righteous; spoil not his resting place:
16 For a just [man] falleth seven times, and riseth
up again: but the wicked shall fall into mischief.
17 Rejoice not when thine enemy falleth, and let
not thine heart be glad when he stumbleth:
18 Lest the LORD see [it], and it displease him, and
he turn away his wrath from him.
19 Fret not thyself because of evil [men], neither be
thou envious at the wicked;
20 For there shall be no reward to the evil [man];
the candle of the wicked shall be put out.
21 My son, fear thou the LORD and the king: [and]
meddle not with them that are given to change:
22 For their calamity shall rise suddenly; and who
knoweth the ruin of them both?
23 These [things] also [belong] to the wise. [It is]
not good to have respect of persons in judgment.
24 He that saith unto the wicked, Thou [art]
righteous; him shall the people curse, nations shall
abhor him:
25 But to them that rebuke [him] shall be delight,
and a good blessing shall come upon them.
26 [Every man] shall kiss [his] lips that giveth a right
answer.
27 Prepare thy work without, and make it fit for

thyself in the field; and afterwards build thine house.
28 Be not a witness against thy neighbour without cause; and deceive [not] with thy lips.
29 Say not, I will do so to him as he hath done to me: I will render to the man according to his work.
30 I went by the field of the slothful, and by the vineyard of the man void of understanding;
31 And, lo, it was all grown over with thorns, [and] nettles had covered the face thereof, and the stone wall thereof was broken down.
32 Then I saw, [and] considered [it] well: I looked upon [it, and] received instruction.
33 [Yet] a little sleep, a little slumber, a little folding of the hands to sleep:
34 So shall thy poverty come [as] one that travelleth; and thy want as an armed man.

Proverbs 25

1 These [are] also proverbs of Solomon, which the men of Hezekiah king of Judah copied out.
2 [It is] the glory of God to conceal a thing: but the honour of kings [is] to search out a matter.
3 The heaven for height, and the earth for depth, and the heart of kings [is] unsearchable.
4 Take away the dross from the silver, and there shall come forth a vessel for the finer.
5 Take away the wicked [from] before the king, and his throne shall be established in righteousness.
6 Put not forth thyself in the presence of the king, and stand not in the place of great [men]:

7 For better [it is] that it be said unto thee, Come
up hither; than that thou shouldest be put lower in
the presence of the prince whom thine eyes have
seen.
8 Go not forth hastily to strive, lest [thou know not]
what to do in the end thereof, when thy neighbour
hath put thee to shame.
9 Debate thy cause with thy neighbour [himself]; and
discover not a secret to another:
10 Lest he that heareth [it] put thee to shame, and
thine infamy turn not away.
11 A word fitly spoken [is like] apples of gold in
pictures of silver.
12 [As] an earring of gold, and an ornament of fine
gold, [so is] a wise reprover upon an obedient ear.
13 As the cold of snow in the time of harvest, [so
is] a faithful messenger to them that send him: for he
refresheth the soul of his masters.
14 Whoso boasteth himself of a false gift [is like]
clouds and wind without rain.
15 By long forbearing is a prince persuaded, and a
soft tongue breaketh the bone.
16 Hast thou found honey? eat so much as is
sufficient for thee, lest thou be filled therewith, and
vomit it.
17 Withdraw thy foot from thy neighbour's house;
lest he be weary of thee, and [so] hate thee.
18 A man that beareth false witness against his
neighbour [is] a maul, and a sword, and a sharp
arrow.

19 Confidence in an unfaithful man in time of trouble [is like] a broken tooth, and a foot out of joint.

20 [As] he that taketh away a garment in cold weather, [and as] vinegar upon nitre, so [is] he that singeth songs to an heavy heart.

21 If thine enemy be hungry, give him bread to eat; and if he be thirsty, give him water to drink:

22 For thou shalt heap coals of fire upon his head, and the LORD shall reward thee.

23 The north wind driveth away rain: so [doth] an angry countenance a backbiting tongue.

24 [It is] better to dwell in the corner of the housetop, than with a brawling woman and in a wide house.

25 [As] cold waters to a thirsty soul, so [is] good news from a far country.

26 A righteous man falling down before the wicked [is as] a troubled fountain, and a corrupt spring.

27 [It is] not good to eat much honey: so [for men] to search their own glory [is not] glory.

28 He that [hath] no rule over his own spirit [is like] a city [that is] broken down, [and] without walls.

Proverbs 26

1 As snow in summer, and as rain in harvest, so honour is not seemly for a fool.

2 As the bird by wandering, as the swallow by flying, so the curse causeless shall not come.

3 A whip for the horse, a bridle for the ass, and a

rod for the fool's back.
4 Answer not a fool according to his folly, lest thou also be like unto him.
5 Answer a fool according to his folly, lest he be wise in his own conceit.
6 He that sendeth a message by the hand of a fool cutteth off the feet, [and] drinketh damage.
7 The legs of the lame are not equal: so [is] a parable in the mouth of fools.
8 As he that bindeth a stone in a sling, so [is] he that giveth honour to a fool.
9 [As] a thorn goeth up into the hand of a drunkard, so [is] a parable in the mouth of fools.
10 The great [God] that formed all [things] both rewardeth the fool, and rewardeth transgressors.
11 As a dog returneth to his vomit, [so] a fool returneth to his folly.
12 Seest thou a man wise in his own conceit? [there is] more hope of a fool than of him.
13 The slothful [man] saith, [There is] a lion in the way; a lion [is] in the streets.
14 [As] the door turneth upon his hinges, so [doth] the slothful upon his bed.
15 The slothful hideth his hand in [his] bosom; it grieveth him to bring it again to his mouth.
16 The sluggard [is] wiser in his own conceit than seven men that can render a reason.
17 He that passeth by, [and] meddleth with strife [belonging] not to him, [is like] one that taketh a dog by the ears.

18 As a mad [man] who casteth firebrands, arrows, and death,
19 So [is] the man [that] deceiveth his neighbour, and saith, Am not I in sport?
20 Where no wood is, [there] the fire goeth out: so where [there is] no talebearer, the strife ceaseth.
21 [As] coals [are] to burning coals, and wood to fire; so [is] a contentious man to kindle strife.
22 The words of a talebearer [are] as wounds, and they go down into the innermost parts of the belly.
23 Burning lips and a wicked heart [are like] a potsherd covered with silver dross.
24 He that hateth dissembleth with his lips, and layeth up deceit within him;
25 When he speaketh fair, believe him not: for [there are] seven abominations in his heart.
26 [Whose] hatred is covered by deceit, his wickedness shall be shewed before the [whole] congregation.
27 Whoso diggeth a pit shall fall therein: and he that rolleth a stone, it will return upon him.
28 A lying tongue hateth [those that are] afflicted by it; and a flattering mouth worketh ruin.

Proverbs 27

1 Boast not thyself of to morrow; for thou knowest not what a day may bring forth.
2 Let another man praise thee, and not thine own mouth; a stranger, and not thine own lips.
3 A stone [is] heavy, and the sand weighty; but a

fool's wrath [is] heavier than them both.
4 Wrath [is] cruel, and anger [is] outrageous; but who [is] able to stand before envy?
5 Open rebuke [is] better than secret love.
6 Faithful [are] the wounds of a friend; but the kisses of an enemy [are] deceitful.
7 The full soul loatheth an honeycomb; but to the hungry soul every bitter thing is sweet.
8 As a bird that wandereth from her nest, so [is] a man that wandereth from his place.
9 Ointment and perfume rejoice the heart: so [doth] the sweetness of a man's friend by hearty counsel.
10 Thine own friend, and thy father's friend, forsake not; neither go into thy brother's house in the day of thy calamity: [for] better [is] a neighbour [that is] near than a brother far off.
11 My son, be wise, and make my heart glad, that I may answer him that reproacheth me.
12 A prudent [man] foreseeth the evil, [and] hideth himself; [but] the simple pass on, [and] are punished.
13 Take his garment that is surety for a stranger, and take a pledge of him for a strange woman.
14 He that blesseth his friend with a loud voice, rising early in the morning, it shall be counted a curse to him.
15 A continual dropping in a very rainy day and a contentious woman are alike.
16 Whosoever hideth her hideth the wind, and the ointment of his right hand, [which] bewrayeth [itself].

17 Iron sharpeneth iron; so a man sharpeneth the countenance of his friend.

18 Whoso keepeth the fig tree shall eat the fruit thereof: so he that waiteth on his master shall be honoured.

19 As in water face [answereth] to face, so the heart of man to man.

20 Hell and destruction are never full; so the eyes of man are never satisfied.

21 [As] the fining pot for silver, and the furnace for gold; so [is] a man to his praise.

22 Though thou shouldest bray a fool in a mortar among wheat with a pestle, [yet] will not his foolishness depart from him.

23 Be thou diligent to know the state of thy flocks, [and] look well to thy herds.

24 For riches [are] not for ever: and doth the crown [endure] to every generation?

25 The hay appeareth, and the tender grass sheweth itself, and herbs of the mountains are gathered.

26 The lambs [are] for thy clothing, and the goats [are] the price of the field.

27 And [thou shalt have] goats' milk enough for thy food, for the food of thy household, and [for] the maintenance for thy maidens.

Proverbs 28

1 The wicked flee when no man pursueth: but the righteous are bold as a lion.

2 For the transgression of a land many [are] the princes thereof: but by a man of understanding [and] knowledge the state [thereof] shall be prolonged.
3 A poor man that oppresseth the poor [is like] a sweeping rain which leaveth no food.
4 They that forsake the law praise the wicked: but such as keep the law contend with them.
5 Evil men understand not judgment: but they that seek the LORD understand all [things].
6 Better [is] the poor that walketh in his uprightness, than [he that is] perverse [in his] ways, though he [be] rich.
7 Whoso keepeth the law [is] a wise son: but he that is a companion of riotous [men] shameth his father.
8 He that by usury and unjust gain increaseth his substance, he shall gather it for him that will pity the poor.
9 He that turneth away his ear from hearing the law, even his prayer [shall be] abomination.
10 Whoso causeth the righteous to go astray in an evil way, he shall fall himself into his own pit: but the upright shall have good [things] in possession.
11 The rich man [is] wise in his own conceit; but the poor that hath understanding searcheth him out.
12 When righteous [men] do rejoice, [there is] great glory: but when the wicked rise, a man is hidden.
13 He that covereth his sins shall not prosper: but whoso confesseth and forsaketh [them] shall have mercy.

14 Happy [is] the man that feareth alway: but he that hardeneth his heart shall fall into mischief.
15 [As] a roaring lion, and a ranging bear; [so is] a wicked ruler over the poor people.
16 The prince that wanteth understanding [is] also a great oppressor: [but] he that hateth covetousness shall prolong [his] days.
17 A man that doeth violence to the blood of [any] person shall flee to the pit; let no man stay him.
18 Whoso walketh uprightly shall be saved: but [he that is] perverse [in his] ways shall fall at once.
19 He that tilleth his land shall have plenty of bread: but he that followeth after vain [persons] shall have poverty enough.
20 A faithful man shall abound with blessings: but he that maketh haste to be rich shall not be innocent.
21 To have respect of persons [is] not good: for for a piece of bread [that] man will transgress.
22 He that hasteth to be rich [hath] an evil eye, and considereth not that poverty shall come upon him.
23 He that rebuketh a man afterwards shall find more favour than he that flattereth with the tongue.
24 Whoso robbeth his father or his mother, and saith, [It is] no transgression; the same [is] the companion of a destroyer.
25 He that is of a proud heart stirreth up strife: but he that putteth his trust in the LORD shall be made fat.
26 He that trusteth in his own heart is a fool: but whoso walketh wisely, he shall be delivered.

27 He that giveth unto the poor shall not lack: but he that hideth his eyes shall have many a curse.
28 When the wicked rise, men hide themselves: but when they perish, the righteous increase.

Proverbs 29

1 He, that being often reproved hardeneth [his] neck, shall suddenly be destroyed, and that without remedy.
2 When the righteous are in authority, the people rejoice: but when the wicked beareth rule, the people mourn.
3 Whoso loveth wisdom rejoiceth his father: but he that keepeth company with harlots spendeth [his] substance.
4 The king by judgment establisheth the land: but he that receiveth gifts overthroweth it.
5 A man that flattereth his neighbour spreadeth a net for his feet.
6 In the transgression of an evil man [there is] a snare: but the righteous doth sing and rejoice.
7 The righteous considereth the cause of the poor: [but] the wicked regardeth not to know [it].
8 Scornful men bring a city into a snare: but wise [men] turn away wrath.
9 [If] a wise man contendeth with a foolish man, whether he rage or laugh, [there is] no rest.
10 The bloodthirsty hate the upright: but the just seek his soul.
11 A fool uttereth all his mind: but a wise [man]

keepeth it in till afterwards.
12 If a ruler hearken to lies, all his servants [are] wicked.
13 The poor and the deceitful man meet together: the LORD lighteneth both their eyes.
14 The king that faithfully judgeth the poor, his throne shall be established for ever.
15 The rod and reproof give wisdom: but a child left [to himself] bringeth his mother to shame.
16 When the wicked are multiplied, transgression increaseth: but the righteous shall see their fall.
17 Correct thy son, and he shall give thee rest; yea, he shall give delight unto thy soul.
18 Where [there is] no vision, the people perish: but he that keepeth the law, happy [is] he.
19 A servant will not be corrected by words: for though he understand he will not answer.
20 Seest thou a man [that is] hasty in his words? [there is] more hope of a fool than of him.
21 He that delicately bringeth up his servant from a child shall have him become [his] son at the length.
22 An angry man stirreth up strife, and a furious man aboundeth in transgression.
23 A man's pride shall bring him low: but honour shall uphold the humble in spirit.
24 Whoso is partner with a thief hateth his own soul: he heareth cursing, and bewrayeth [it] not.
25 The fear of man bringeth a snare: but whoso putteth his trust in the LORD shall be safe.
26 Many seek the ruler's favour; but [every] man's

judgment [cometh] from the LORD.
27 An unjust man [is] an abomination to the just: and [he that is] upright in the way [is] abomination to the wicked.

Proverbs 30

1 The words of Agur the son of Jakeh, [even] the prophecy: the man spake unto Ithiel, even unto Ithiel and Ucal,
2 Surely I [am] more brutish than [any] man, and have not the understanding of a man.
3 I neither learned wisdom, nor have the knowledge of the holy.
4 Who hath ascended up into heaven, or descended? who hath gathered the wind in his fists? who hath bound the waters in a garment? who hath established all the ends of the earth? what [is] his name, and what [is] his son's name, if thou canst tell?
5 Every word of God [is] pure: he [is] a shield unto them that put their trust in him.
6 Add thou not unto his words, lest he reprove thee, and thou be found a liar.
7 Two [things] have I required of thee; deny me [them] not before I die:
8 Remove far from me vanity and lies: give me neither poverty nor riches; feed me with food convenient for me:
9 Lest I be full, and deny [thee], and say, Who [is] the LORD? or lest I be poor, and steal, and take the name of my God [in vain].

10 Accuse not a servant unto his master, lest he
curse thee, and thou be found guilty.
11 [There is] a generation [that] curseth their
father, and doth not bless their mother.
12 [There is] a generation [that are] pure in their
own eyes, and [yet] is not washed from their
filthiness.
13 [There is] a generation, O how lofty are their
eyes! and their eyelids are lifted up.
14 [There is] a generation, whose teeth [are as]
swords, and their jaw teeth [as] knives, to devour the
poor from off the earth, and the needy from [among]
men.
15 The horseleach hath two daughters, [crying],
Give, give. There are three [things that] are never
satisfied, [yea], four [things] say not, [It is] enough:
16 The grave; and the barren womb; the earth
[that] is not filled with water; and the fire [that] saith
not, [It is] enough.
17 The eye [that] mocketh at [his] father, and
despiseth to obey [his] mother, the ravens of the
valley shall pick it out, and the young eagles shall eat
it.
18 There be three [things which] are too wonderful
for me, yea, four which I know not:
19 The way of an eagle in the air; the way of a
serpent upon a rock; the way of a ship in the midst
of the sea; and the way of a man with a maid.
20 Such [is] the way of an adulterous woman; she
eateth, and wipeth her mouth, and saith, I have done

no wickedness.
21 For three [things] the earth is disquieted, and for
four [which] it cannot bear:
22 For a servant when he reigneth; and a fool when
he is filled with meat;
23 For an odious [woman] when she is married; and
an handmaid that is heir to her mistress.
24 There be four [things which are] little upon the
earth, but they [are] exceeding wise:
25 The ants [are] a people not strong, yet they
prepare their meat in the summer;
26 The conies [are but] a feeble folk, yet make they
their houses in the rocks;
27 The locusts have no king, yet go they forth all of
them by bands;
28 The spider taketh hold with her hands, and is in
kings' palaces.
29 There be three [things] which go well, yea, four
are comely in going:
30 A lion [which is] strongest among beasts, and
turneth not away for any;
31 A greyhound; an he goat also; and a king, against
whom [there is] no rising up.
32 If thou hast done foolishly in lifting up thyself, or
if thou hast thought evil, [lay] thine hand upon thy
mouth.
33 Surely the churning of milk bringeth forth butter,
and the wringing of the nose bringeth forth blood: so
the forcing of wrath bringeth forth strife.

Proverbs 31

1 The words of king Lemuel, the prophecy that his
mother taught him.
2 What, my son? and what, the son of my womb?
and what, the son of my vows?
3 Give not thy strength unto women, nor thy ways
to that which destroyeth kings.
4 [It is] not for kings, O Lemuel, [it is] not for kings
to drink wine; nor for princes strong drink:
5 Lest they drink, and forget the law, and pervert the
judgment of any of the afflicted.
6 Give strong drink unto him that is ready to perish,
and wine unto those that be of heavy hearts.
7 Let him drink, and forget his poverty, and
remember his misery no more.
8 Open thy mouth for the dumb in the cause of all
such as are appointed to destruction.
9 Open thy mouth, judge righteously, and plead the
cause of the poor and needy.
10 Who can find a virtuous woman? for her price
[is] far above rubies.
11 The heart of her husband doth safely trust in
her, so that he shall have no need of spoil.
12 She will do him good and not evil all the days of
her life.
13 She seeketh wool, and flax, and worketh
willingly with her hands.
14 She is like the merchants' ships; she bringeth her
food from afar.

15 She riseth also while it is yet night, and giveth
meat to her household, and a portion to her maidens.
16 She considereth a field, and buyeth it: with the
fruit of her hands she planteth a vineyard.
17 She girdeth her loins with strength, and
strengtheneth her arms.
18 She perceiveth that her merchandise [is] good:
her candle goeth not out by night.
19 She layeth her hands to the spindle, and her
hands hold the distaff.
20 She stretcheth out her hand to the poor; yea,
she reacheth forth her hands to the needy.
21 She is not afraid of the snow for her household:
for all her household [are] clothed with scarlet.
22 She maketh herself coverings of tapestry; her
clothing [is] silk and purple.
23 Her husband is known in the gates, when he
sitteth among the elders of the land.
24 She maketh fine linen, and selleth [it]; and
delivereth girdles unto the merchant.
25 Strength and honour [are] her clothing; and she
shall rejoice in time to come.
26 She openeth her mouth with wisdom; and in her
tongue [is] the law of kindness.
27 She looketh well to the ways of her household,
and eateth not the bread of idleness.
28 Her children arise up, and call her blessed; her
husband [also], and he praiseth her.
29 Many daughters have done virtuously, but thou
excellest them all.

30 Favour [is] deceitful, and beauty [is] vain: [but] a
woman [that] feareth the LORD, she shall be praised.
31 Give her of the fruit of her hands; and let her
own works praise her in the gates.

Printed in Great Britain
by Amazon

60929553R00043